Kitchen Garden Cookbook: *Potatoes*

Jane McMorland Hunter

🍂 National Trust

To David Piachaud

First published in the United Kingdom in 2011 by National Trust Books,
10 Southcombe Street, London W14 0RA

An imprint of Anova Books Company Ltd

ISBN 978 1 907892 02 8

A CIP catalogue record for this book is available from the British Library.

19 18 17 16 15 14 13 12
10 9 8 7 6 5 4 3 2 1

Reproduction by Mission Productions, Hong Kong
Printed and bound by 1010 Printing International, China

Acknowledgements

Louy, David, Lily and Toby Piachaud; Sue and David Gibb; Kate and Aimi
Engineer; Deborah Cowles; Libby Kerr; Vanessa Wagstaff; Sally Hughes;
and all at Books for Cooks have variously supplied recipes, tested them
and tasted the finished products. Without them, the recipe section of this
book would have been about half the size and a lot less accurate. Chris
Kelly has helped with the growing and history sections, and Paul Honor
has helped with everything else. Teresa Chris has, as always, been the
perfect agent: enthusiastic and encouraging. Grant Berry, the staff at the
National Trust gardens and the RHS library at Wisley made the research
fun and easy. At Anova Books, Tina Persaud, Nicola Newman and Komal
Patel have been brilliant to work with. Finally, a huge thanks to Tony
Smith and Aimi Engineer at Slightly Foxed for coping with the fact that
for some time all I have wanted to talk about is potatoes.

Contents

Introduction

For too long, potatoes were the unsung heroes of both
the vegetable garden and the kitchen. Everyone grew
them because they were easy, and everyone ate them
because they acted as ballast for so many dishes. People
didn't really consider which variety they were eating
and only Jersey Royals ever received any praise.

When potatoes were first introduced into Europe,
many people weren't sure what they were, calling them
earth truffles or earth apples in an attempt to link them
with a food they recognised. They were mistrusted as a
reliable food, and people preferred wheat as their
staple. In the nineteenth century, a group called the
Society for the Prevention of Unwholesome Diet even
tried to ban potatoes in Britain.

The name 'spud' originally referred to a short knife
in the fifteenth century, then a digging tool, then a fork
with three flat tines or prongs that was used for
planting and harvesting potatoes, and it finally became
the colloquial name for potatoes in the mid-nineteenth
century. From mid-Victorian times onwards, potatoes
gained popularity as entries on the show bench at
garden fêtes and shows, but these vegetables were
grown purely for looks and no one would have dreamt of
judging them by taste.

All that has now changed, and
today we have a huge variety
of potatoes to choose from.
Heritage varieties preserve
the history of the garden and
coloured ones provide

entertainment at the table. Potatoes, and the dishes you can cook with them, reflect the seasons in just the same way as asparagus and strawberries. Certainly, you can buy 'new' potatoes in November, but surely one of the charms of autumn and winter is big, hearty baked potatoes or fluffy mash? If you grow your own potatoes, you will appreciate the subtle changes in them as the year progresses and, as this book shows, you only need a tiny space to get a very satisfactory crop.

Although potatoes originally came from the High Andes, they have adapted to the European climate. Britain is the perfect place to grow them; nowhere is too hot, too cold, too dry or too damp. Whatever the conditions in your area, there will be a variety you can cultivate successfully. You then have a wealth of recipes to choose from.

Until fairly recently, you would not have visited a garden to look at the vegetables. Flowers, shrubs and lawns formed the display areas, with the kitchen garden hidden away. In the early part of the twentieth century, labour-intensive kitchen gardens became increasingly difficult to look after and many were grassed over or filled with flowers and shrubs. Now these gardens are being restored to their former glory: up and down the country National Trust properties boast kitchen gardens that are both practical and inspirational, and are often used to feed visitors in on-site restaurants.

The potato is packed with potential. It may seem ordinary, but that does not make it any less important. Technology can give us many things, but the latest electronic gizmo cannot compare with a helping of chips.

A brief history of potatoes

The humble potato has had a chequered history, from being reviled as the food of the Devil to bringing about the rise and fall of nations.

Ancient origins

The potato we know today (*Solanum tuberosum*) originated in South America some 8,000 years ago. Over 200 species still grow wild high in the Peruvian Andes, above the line where corn will survive. The tubers tend to be small, knobbly and misshapen and come in a rainbow of colours: blue, black, purple and red are as common as white or yellow. In 5000 BC, hunter-gatherers moved west from the Amazon jungle on to the plateau around Lake Titicaca, on what is now the border between Peru and Bolivia. They discovered potatoes, at first eating them raw and later cooked. Ancient fragments of pottery, 4,000 years old, show that potatoes may have been worshipped as well as eaten. Pottery vessels in the shape of potatoes with deep eyes, dating from AD 1000, indicate that potatoes were being cultivated by this time.

Potatoes arrive in Europe

In 1537, Spanish adventurers found 'truffles' in an Andean village in what is now Columbia. Clearly edible, they were brought back to Europe, although exactly when is uncertain. Part of the confusion arises from the fact that until 1770, the term 'potato' was used to refer to potatoes, sweet potatoes and yams. By 1576, potatoes were fairly widely grown in Spain and from here they gradually spread to the rest of mainland Europe.

At first, this new vegetable was greeted with suspicion. The flowers were remarkably similar to deadly nightshade (the potato is part of the same family), which everyone knew was poisonous. All parts of the plant except the tubers are poisonous, and when some people ate the leaves and seeds and became ill or died, it added to the potato's negative image. Also, everyone was managing perfectly well without potatoes: bread was considered the most important staple, and grain made better bread. The lumpy tubers were thought to cause leprosy as it seemed that eating them raw could bring on eczema, which looked similar. Finally, the fact that they grew underground was considered unnatural, and many regarded potatoes as the food of the Devil.

England and America

Potatoes were probably brought to England by the naval commander Sir John Hawkins in 1563. Twenty years later, his relation Sir Francis Drake brought more, which he may have found during raids on Spanish ships. Again, potatoes got off to a shaky start. Sir Walter Raleigh's chef served the leaves rather than the tubers at a banquet. Sixteenth-century England was a very religious place and potatoes were viewed with deep suspicion; their curvy shapes seemed questionably seductive and they were not mentioned in the Bible.

Even potato supporters managed to cause confusion: John Gerard praised them in his Herbal of 1596, but referred to them as 'potatoes of Virginia' (Sir Francis Drake did have colonists from Virginia on board his ship, but had probably collected the potatoes with stores from the Caribbean on his voyage home. Potatoes did not reach North America until 1621, when they were introduced by the Pilgrim Fathers). Gerard provided great publicity for the potato, being pictured on the frontispiece of his herbal holding a spray of potato flowers, yet no one knew where they came from, which parts to eat or how to cook them. Over a hundred years later, in 1699, there was still confusion when John Evelyn appeared to recommend not only the roots, but also the fruits, pickled, in his *Acetaria: A Discourse of Sallets*.

Gradually, the potato became accepted in Britain; planting on Good Friday with holy water was recommended, with cooks then 'boiling the Devil out of them'. Once established, they spread rapidly. In 1728, cultivation was forbidden in Scotland as they were not mentioned in the Bible, whereas by the time Samuel Johnson visited the Highlands in 1773, they were everywhere: 'Potatoes are at least never wanting, which, though they have not known them long, are now one of the principal parts of their food.'

The Irish famine

The most infamous event in the potato's history must be the Great Famine of 1845 in Ireland. Most estimates agree that during the 1840s at least 1.5 million Irish people died and a further million emigrated as a result of failed potato harvests. What is less well known is that the potato had supported an enormous population increase in Ireland in the preceding years, far beyond the level that the land could realistically support. The population had risen steeply from 1.5 million in 1760 to 9 million in 1840.

Potatoes may have been washed up on the Irish coast from the ships of the Spanish Armada, or Sir Walter Raleigh may have introduced them on his Irish estates. Either way, by the end of the eighteenth century, one-third of the population relied almost exclusively on potatoes. An old Irish proverb recommends: 'Be eating one potato, peeling a second, have a third in your fist, and your eye on a fourth.' They were boiled in seawater and delivered to the table in a wooden bowl, or silver basket if you were a member of the aristocracy. During lean times, meals were described as 'potato and point' – you ate potatoes and pointed at the bacon hanging in the rafters.

Cultivation was extremely easy. Most Irish used the lazy-bed method, which would feed a family for almost

no effort. You simply piled manure of any type on to an area of land, dug a trench around it and piled the soil on top, creating a raised bed. The potatoes were planted in this and the bed could later be used for storage. Crop rotation was unheard of and the only variety cultivated was the 'Lumper', famous for producing extremely dull potatoes in huge quantities. Unfortunately the Lumper was susceptible to blight, a disease that can wipe out a crop almost overnight.

Potato blight appeared in Belgium in the 1830s, probably from the Americas or Mexico, and spread around Europe, reaching Ireland in 1845. The problem in Ireland was that most of the poor existed on the brink of starvation. More than half the population had never had any contact with money and were unable to buy any alternative food when their crops failed. Many of the landlords were absentee English Protestants and most did nothing to alleviate the sufferings of their largely Catholic tenants. In desperation, many Irish people fled the country. America was one of the main destinations, and ancestors of the Kennedys and Ronald Reagan were amongst the emigrants.

New varieties

The Irish famine alerted the Victorians to the need to improve the strains of potato. In South America, potatoes thrive in thin soils, with short days, low night temperatures and little rain. In Europe they grow in richer soil, with long days, warm nights and moist weather – conditions that unfortunately favour blight. Scotland became a major area for breeding potatoes, its cooler climate reducing the risk of disease. Many new varieties were introduced during the latter years of the nineteenth century, including Duke of York and Epicure, which are still popular today.

In 1947, potatoes were rationed for the first time as a result of the Second World War. This possibly led people to appreciate them more, rather than simply regarding them as a staple that was always readily available. Whatever the reason, people took a new interest in potatoes in the second half of the twentieth century. Increasingly, they gained status as 'an interesting food', new varieties were bred and old ones rescued from oblivion. Potatoes were finally grown for their individual flavours, colours and looks rather than simply as a means of survival.

In 1995, potatoes were the first vegetable to be grown in space and research has shown that they would be the easiest vegetable to grow on Mars.

Uses for potatoes

In South America, the potato was worshipped and credited with medicinal and even magical powers, but in Europe it never really gained such an exalted status. Like many new and exotic species, it was rumoured to be an aphrodisiac and in sixteenth-century Spain, the value of potatoes soared when they were thought to cure impotence.

At one time, it was widely believed that carrying a potato in your pocket eased rheumatism, lumbago and toothache – it was believed to somehow absorb some of the acid in the body, and it was always stated that the

cure would be more effective if the potato had been stolen. Drinking potato juice, or the water potatoes were cooked in, was also thought to help. Warts were said to disappear if you rubbed them with a slice of potato and then buried it, and, more believably, raw potatoes, peeled and crushed to a paste, eased burns.

Potatoes also have cleansing powers. In the nineteenth century potato starch powder was used to whiten wigs, and the juice of a mature potato will clean fabrics and polished surfaces. Since the seventeenth century, potatoes have been made into bird-scarers; long white feathers were stuck into the tubers, which were then hung in the vegetable garden. These resembled hawks and frightened away pigeons eating the crops.

Potatoes
in the
garden

Growing potatoes

Potatoes are one of the easiest and most rewarding vegetables to grow: you simply put a seed potato in the soil, give the plant a little care and, a few months later, you have the joy of digging down and unearthing meal after meal of potatoes, which taste a million times better than their shop-bought counterparts. That is, of course, a simplification, but not as much of one as you might imagine.

Potatoes are perennials, but are best grown as annuals in the UK as they are half-hardy. They dislike cold and cannot survive frost. In growing terms, they are divided into three groups: first earlies, second earlies and maincrop potatoes. The dividing lines are not exact and you may find a particular variety in a different group according to supplier. Maincrop potatoes can be further divided into early and late.

These divisions refer to how long the potato takes to grow and are not an indication of texture, size, colour or taste. The timings given below are a rough guide and obviously depend on local factors such as weather, soil, aspect and the temperature of the soil at the time of planting. Also, timings can be played with – for example, you can grow first earlies under cover for an early crop, and you can also plant them late for a crop of new potatoes to enjoy on Christmas Day.

First earlies

First earlies grow fastest, take up less space than the other two groups, give smaller yields of smaller potatoes, and are less prone to problems such as blight. They should be planted out in mid-spring and harvested in early summer to midsummer, spending 10–14 weeks in the ground. First earlies include most waxy or salad potatoes, some floury ones and all new potatoes, of which Jersey Royals are probably the most famous.

16

New potatoes are harvested before they are fully grown and their most recognisable characteristic is a flaking skin, which can be pulled or rubbed away. Some of them, such as International Kidney (which is a Jersey Royal grown anywhere other than Jersey), will grow into larger, floury potatoes if left in the ground.

First earlies are the potatoes to grow if you don't have much space, and will even grow perfectly well in containers. This is also the group that is most obviously better when home-grown. A new potato tastes its best when dug from the ground and taken straight into the kitchen; a home-grown maincrop floury potato used for mash may not taste so different to one bought from a greengrocer. First earlies tend to be the least susceptible to disease. They give small yields of small potatoes, but that is exactly what you want – they don't store well and need to be eaten straight away. If you stagger the sowing over a month, you will get a longer harvest of perfect potatoes.

Second earlies

Second earlies bridge the gap between first earlies and maincrop potatoes and are sometimes called mid-crop potatoes. They should be planted in mid-spring and harvested in midsummer to early autumn, having spent 15–17 weeks in the ground. This group includes potatoes of all shapes and textures – small, large, waxy and floury – so choose carefully. Some varieties have better disease resistance than others and you may need to take this into account.

Juin

BINAGE DES PO^mes DE T^re

Maincrop potatoes

Maincrop potatoes take up more space and are more prone to pests and diseases than the first two groups. This is partly because they are in the soil longer – typically 18–22 weeks. They are also growing during the hot (and often damp) late summer months, which are ideal for the spread of disease. However, you get higher yields per plant and the potatoes will store well, lasting right through to the following year's new season. Most of the floury potatoes are in this group, but also some delicious waxy or salad potatoes that mature late in the season, such as Pink Fir Apple. Maincrops should be planted out in mid-spring for harvesting in early to late autumn.

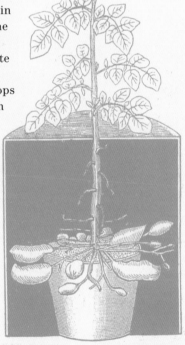

Site and soil

All potatoes need an airy, frost-free site, in full sun if
possible. In terms of soil they are not that fussy, but
you will get a better crop in a slightly acidic soil
(pH 5–6), which is rich and moisture-retentive. You can
help to ensure these conditions by digging well-rotted
manure or compost into the soil the previous autumn.
Avoid waterlogged sites and if the soil is very free-
draining, choose drought-tolerant varieties such as
Desirée, Estima or Picasso.

Potatoes can be used to break up soil, especially
areas that have been compacted under grassland or
left to run wild. The harvest will not be brilliant, but the
plants will loosen the soil for you and the area can be
used for vegetables the following year. The vigorous
foliage will also help to suppress any weeds.

Crop rotation

Whatever vegetables you grow, it is vital to rotate the
crops. This has the double benefit of reducing the risk
of disease and ensuring that the soil does not become
exhausted. Most sites are not uniformly ideal for all
crops and you will probably not be able to practise
perfect crop rotation. The important thing is to rotate
the crops as much as you can: as a rough guide, early
potatoes should not be grown in the same spot more
than one year in three, and maincrops not more than
one year in five.

A good three-year rotation plan would be potatoes
and root vegetables, followed by legumes and then

brassicas. If you want a decent amount of potatoes and have the space, you can grow them on their own, ahead of the root vegetables. By growing vegetables in this order, you will actually replenish the nutrients in the soil over the years, rather than exhaust them. The legumes release nitrogen into the soil, which will provide food for the brassicas. After harvesting the brassicas, you can compost the area in autumn ready for the potatoes the following spring. The potatoes will then break up the soil, making it easy for the legumes to grow. It is extremely unlikely that you can carry out a perfect rotation system, particularly if you grow vegetables amongst flowers and other ornamentals, but any movement is better than none.

Preparation

The amount of preparation you do will, to a certain
extent, determine the success of your crop. For a really
good crop, dig well-rotted manure or compost into the
soil the previous autumn. This will give it time to break
up properly before you start planting in the spring.
Avoid mushroom compost or any mixture containing
lime, as this will increase the risk of scab (a bacterial
disease that affects appearance). Over winter, leave the
area roughly dug so that the rain and frost can get into
the soil and further break it up. In spring, level the site
so that it is ready for planting. Rake over and ten days
before planting, add a general fertiliser.

An alternative is to create raised beds for your
potatoes. Use planks or woven hurdles to create the
walls of a bed 1.5m (5ft) wide. This width ensures that
you will be able to reach across the bed without
stepping on the soil. It does not matter how long the bed
is. Dig the bottom if it is very compacted and fill with a
mixture of soil and compost, or well-rotted manure. This
is a variation on the lazy-bed scheme that was common
first in South America and later in Ireland.

Getting started

The tubers we eat are actually swollen stems, not roots, and this is why they grow shoots. Potato plants are best grown from seed potatoes, which are specially bred. These should be certified 'virus-free' and are easily available in late winter and early spring. If you opt for well-known varieties, you will be able to buy them at a nursery or garden centre, but the best places to see a really wide selection are at the Potato Days held by various organizations (see page 94) or in the mail-order catalogues of specialist growers. It may be possible to buy small quantities or mixed bags, so you are not stuck with a large quantity of a single variety. A word of warning: if you want particular varieties, order them early as many suppliers have limited quantities.

You can also buy micro-plants or plantlets. These are small, virus-free plants, which you buy and plant out in the same way as seed potatoes, once any danger of frost has past. This is often the best way to obtain some of the more unusual and heritage varieties.

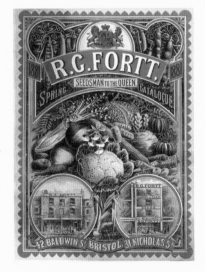

The flowers of potato plants produce poisonous seeds that look like small tomatoes. Many varieties available now do not produce fertile seed, but some will grow into potato plants. This is a rather hit-and-miss method of propagation and seed potatoes are a much more reliable way of ensuring a decent crop. Do not be tempted to plant shop-bought potatoes, even if they have started to sprout in your vegetable rack. These potatoes may contain viruses, which will not harm you if you eat them, but could spread in the soil if planted and cause long-term problems.

Chitting

This process encourages the seed potato to produce shoots before it is planted in the ground. Gardeners are divided as to whether it is worth the trouble, with one camp saying all seed potatoes should be chitted and the other saying that it is a waste of time. On balance, it probably is worth chitting first and second earlies. It gives them a head start and will give you a quicker crop of smaller potatoes – which is exactly what you want. As maincrop potatoes are in the ground longer, getting them off to a quick start matters less. Another point in favour of chitting is that it is very simple to do and can be carried out when nothing much else is happening in the garden.

When the seed potatoes arrive, place them in trays, with the largest eyes or sprouts pointing upwards. This is called the rose end. Egg boxes are ideal for wedging the potatoes upright, or you can put them in shallow trays with strips of rolled-up newspaper to hold them in position. The potatoes need to be kept somewhere light, but out of direct sunlight, and it should be cool but frost-free, ideally about 10°C (50°F). Spare-room window-sills are ideal. After about six weeks, the potatoes should have grown shoots 2.5cm (1in) long. You don't want the shoots to get much longer than this, as they are delicate and will tend to break off. If you leave all the shoots on, you will get a high yield of small potatoes; removing all but three will give you fewer, larger potatoes.

Planting

There are various traditional days for planting potatoes. Good Friday was a popular date historically, partly because, growing underground, potatoes were regarded

as the Devil's food and planting them on Good Friday was felt to counter this and render them acceptable to eat. It was also one of the few days that farmworkers would have had free to work on their own plots. The downside of choosing Good Friday is that the date of Easter moves, and in a year when it is early, many areas could still be at risk of frost. St Patrick's Day (17 March) was another popular day, but is probably a bit early in all but sheltered gardens.

The most important thing is that the soil should be warm and the risk of frost should have passed before the shoots appear above ground. It is much better to plant potatoes too late than too early. It is hard to tell exactly when you should plant seed potatoes, but about one month before you expect the last frost is usually safe (i.e. if you don't usually get frost after the beginning of May, you can safely plant in early April). You can plant earlies in advance of this, but you will need to use cloches or black plastic for protection (see 'Forcing an early crop of earlies', page 31). Stagger the planting of earlies at two-weekly intervals: they don't keep well and this will give you a longer season of delicious, fresh new potatoes. Maincrops keep perfectly well, so they can go in all at the same time.

Depending on whereabouts you are planting and the number of potatoes you have to plant, you can either dig trenches or individual holes. If you are planting rows – and have the option – align them north to south, so each side of the plant receives an equal amount of sunshine.

All seed potatoes should be planted 7–15cm (3–6in) deep. For first earlies, the spacings should be 30–38cm

(12–15in) between plants and
38–50cm (15–20in) between
rows. For second earlies and
maincrops, the spacings
should be 38cm (15in)
between plants
and 75cm (30in)
between rows.

The extra space between
the later crops allows the air to
circulate through the plants (thereby
reducing the risk of disease) and gives
the plants room to grow, so the potatoes can
develop properly (early potatoes can be planted closer
together as the risk of disease is not as high early in the
year, and it doesn't matter if the plants are a bit
restricted as you want small potatoes anyway). The
spacing for the later crops may seem wide when you
plant the seed potatoes, but remember that each one
you put into the ground will turn into many more.

Dig the hole or trench a bit deeper than you need and
add a layer of well-rotted manure, compost, seaweed,
grass clippings or comfrey leaves. All will improve the
texture of the soil and help prevent scab; what you use
will probably depend on what is easiest to obtain.
Comfrey leaves contain a high concentration of
beneficial potassium and should be wilted or torn up.
Next, add a thin layer of soil and place the seed potatoes
on this with the rose end pointing upwards. Cover the
potatoes with soil and water gently.

Care

Frost protection

Ideally, rule out worries about frost by planting the seed potatoes sufficiently late in the year. A frost will slow the rate of growth, whereas late-planted seed potatoes have the benefit of warmer soil and air, and will grow more strongly and rapidly. If you expect a late frost, you can protect the young plants with fleece, plastic or cloches. To protect the haulm (stem and foliage) of large plants, wrap gently with newspaper or straw. Light frosts shouldn't matter and a few frosted leaves aren't a problem, but a heavy frost could kill the plant and will certainly retard its growth.

Earthing up

The process of 'earthing up' shields potatoes from light (essential to prevent poisonous green potatoes), and provides protection from frost and some defence against blight. It also gives them soft, easy soil to grow in.

When the plants are 15–20cm (6–8in) tall, spread a handful of fish, blood and bone or well-rotted organic matter around the base and pull the surrounding soil up and around the stem until only the top 8–10cm (3–4in) is showing. A draw hoe is the easiest tool to use for this. Earth up every 2–3 weeks, until the leaves start spreading out.

Weeding

Weed gently around the potatoes at first, using a hoe. This will clear away the competitive weeds without disturbing the potatoes. Earthing up will disturb the weeds and once the potato leaves are growing, they will cut off the supply of light to the ground and so you should not need to weed at all.

Watering

Potatoes need a constant supply of water in order to grow properly. Give earlies 16–22 litres per square metre (3–5 gallons per square yard) every 1–2 weeks, depending on the weather and soil type. Maincrops don't need watering until the tubers are about the size of a marble. You can feel their size by gently digging around in the soil with your fingertips. At this point, the plants do better with a thorough soaking rather than more frequent sprinkling.

Regular watering offers protection against scab and ensures that the potatoes grow at a constant pace. It is vitally important to provide ample water once the plants come into flower, as this shows that the tubers are swelling beneath the ground. Water between the rows, rather than watering the plants directly. The water will soak down to the tubers without disturbing the earthed-up soil, and the plants will remain healthier if you don't sprinkle too much water on the stem and foliage.

Feeding

An organic liquid feed or nitrogen-based top dressing will help the plants establish themselves. Potatoes need a good supply of potassium and if the soil is free-draining, it may get washed away. Wood ash and comfrey are good sources of potassium and can be dug in or used as a mulch. You can also use liquid food – one designed for tomatoes (which also need potassium) or one made from comfrey. Potatoes that are planted in well-prepared soil shouldn't need much extra food.

The black plastic method

This is an unsightly but highly efficient way of growing potatoes. Prepare the soil in early spring as you would for ordinary planting, but then cover the entire area with black plastic, fixing it along the edges with soil or stones. This will suppress any weeds and warm the soil beneath. Simply cut crosses in the plastic, dig a shallow hole and insert the seed potatoes with the rose end upwards as before. The plastic cancels the need to earth up and protects the tubers from the light. The crop will be easy to look after and ready to harvest slightly earlier, but this method will not enhance the appearance of your garden!

The no-dig method

You need to start off with a clear area of soil, so you
may need to dig the ground when you initially clear it.
Rake the ground flat and then cover it with a layer of
well-rotted manure or compost. Space the seed potatoes
as you would for conventional planting, placing them
with the rose end uppermost. Cover with a 5–8cm
(2–3in) layer of straw, hay, compost or leaf mould,
adding more as the shoots grow up, until the top layer is
about 15cm (6in) deep. Then spread an 8–10cm (3–4in)
layer of lawn cuttings on top to weigh it down and cut
out any light. This system is easy and produces a good
crop, but it is not attractive and depends on your having
sufficient compost, or easy access to hay or straw.

Forcing an early crop of earlies

If you want an early crop of new potatoes in late spring,
choose one of the quick-growing varieties such as Swift
or Mimi. Buy the seed potatoes as soon as you can in
late winter, and put them to chit. Once the shoots are
6mm (½in) long, plant them out.

Choose a mild day in early spring. Fill a 38cm (15in)
container with a mixture of multipurpose compost and
specialist vegetable compost, and plant three seed
potatoes at a depth of 13cm (5in). Keep in a frost-free
greenhouse, making sure there is plenty of light.
Stake the haulms if they look wobbly. If you use a rigid
container, you can move it outside once the weather
warms up. Feed and water regularly, and the potatoes
should be ready to harvest a good month before normal.

Growing a late crop of earlies for Christmas

Winter is a time for the comfort of roast potatoes and mash, but a serving of new potatoes at Christmas is a delightful novelty, if only to remind us that the cold weather does not last for ever and that the new potato season is only a few months away. In supermarkets it is possible to buy 'new' potatoes almost all year round, but the ones you grow at home will be the real thing and will taste very different.

Many suppliers sell early seed potatoes late in the season specifically for this purpose. They will have been kept dormant in cold storage, but you can do much the same at home. Keep back a few of earlies and, once they have sprouted, put each one in a 15cm (6in) pot and bury it in multipurpose compost to the tip of the tallest shoot. Keep watered and plant out in midsummer, into a container at least 30cm (12in) in diameter and 60cm (24in) deep. Feed and water regularly, and earth up as you would for any container-grown plant (see Growing potatoes in containers, page 34).

At the start of autumn, move the container to a sheltered spot or an unheated greenhouse. If you have room, you can put the plants straight into a bed in a frost-free greenhouse. During autumn, the upper growth will largely cease. Cover with a mulch of straw to protect from frost and harvest on or around Christmas Day. You won't get a huge harvest, but that is not the point – the taste of new potatoes in the depths of winter is what you are after. Charlotte and Maris Peer are good varieties for Christmas new potatoes.

Potatoes as ornamentals

Potatoes are not necessarily the first vegetables that spring to mind as ornamentals. Maincrop potatoes, in particular, look messy as they die down and all potatoes leave an unsightly gap when they are harvested. However, there is an energetic and vigorous air about the plants, and although the flowers are small, many are very pretty, coming in shades of pink, blue, mauve and white. In 1658 Olaus Rudbeck of Uppsala, who established the first botanic garden in Sweden, described potatoes as 'equally suitable for the flower border and the table', and their road towards acceptance in France was greatly helped when Louis XVI and Marie Antoinette wore the flowers.

Most potato plants reach 30–75cm (12–30in) in height and are about 60–100cm (2–3ft) wide. They are perfect for the back of a border and when you harvest earlies, you can fill the gap with late-flowering annuals such as cosmos or dahlias. Maris Peer is an attractive plant with pretty purple flowers. Ratte has purple flowers with brilliant yellow centres. Charlotte has reddish-violet flowers; Duke of York and Red Duke of York have white flowers. Desirée, Mimi, Ratte and Swift are compact plants; Golden Wonder, Kerr's Pink and Roseval are tall.

Growing potatoes in containers

You can grow potatoes almost anywhere, even on a balcony, if you use containers. You won't achieve a huge harvest, but you will get several delicious meals and the statuesque plants can look very good at the back of a group of containers.

Types of container

The smallest size of container that is practical for potatoes is 30cm (12in) wide and 60cm (24in) deep, though it may only give you a single meal of potatoes. Regardless of the size, drainage holes are vital to prevent waterlogging, as is a pot made out of a dark, opaque material, so that no light reaches the tubers.

Potato barrels are purpose-made containers with side panels that slide open so that you can harvest some potatoes without disturbing the rest. Problems may arise because they are very deep and the lower levels can become compacted, reducing the harvest.

Plastic bags are an unsightly but practical way to grow potatoes. Pierce holes around the bottom of the bag and roll the sides down the outside until the bag is about 15cm (6in) tall. When the potatoes need earthing up, you simply roll up the bag and add more compost. Old potting-compost bags are good and some are even quite attractive: one brand has a pattern of leaves on the bag.

Tyres are another practical container, but they have to be positioned carefully and disguised, or your garden

will look like a spare parts yard. Start with two tyres and add more as you earth up. You can build a tower up to five tyres high, and then simply dismantle it when you want to harvest the potatoes.

One of the most practical and attractive containers is a purpose-made bag with removable wicker side panels. This will give you a good crop (a standard square one takes five seed potatoes) and can be packed away in the winter so the wicker won't disintegrate (see page 35).

Really, any well-drained, opaque container of a decent size will do perfectly well.

Planting and care

One of the difficulties of planting in containers is the fact that you only want to buy a small number of seed potatoes and suppliers often sell in larger quantities. Keep an eye out at nurseries or on Potato Days (see page 94) for suppliers who are selling single seed potatoes.

Alternatively, get together with some friends, buy a mixed bag of potatoes and share them out.

The container you use must have drainage holes and should, ideally, be raised off the ground on feet or bricks. Position it in full sun. Shade will result in lanky plants and poor harvests. If you want a very early harvest, start the container off in a greenhouse in early spring and move it outside once there is no risk of frost.

Put a 5–8cm (2–3in) layer of grit at the bottom of the container to ensure that it drains properly. Add 5–8cm (2–3in) of compost and water gently so the compost settles and is damp. You can use multipurpose compost or specialist vegetable compost. Put the potatoes into the compost, the rose end pointing upwards, and add more compost so the top shoot is just covered. The potatoes should be 20cm (8in) apart. A deep pot, 30cm (12in) in diameter, will take one seed potato; one with a diameter of 45cm (18in) will take three. By putting the seed potatoes at the bottom of the container, you get a bigger harvest, as potatoes will be produced throughout the depth of the container. The dense planting will give you small tubers, but with containers you are aiming for quality rather than quantity anyway.

When the stems are 15cm (6in) tall, add more compost until just the tips are showing. Water regularly, so the compost is always damp. Continue adding compost as the plants grow, until they reach 5cm (2in) below the rim of the container. Once the flower buds appear, feed once a week with tomato food or liquid comfrey.

If you plant first earlies, you can plant a second crop for later in the season. Either hold back some seed

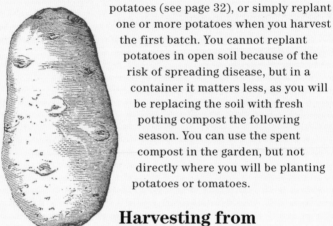

potatoes (see page 32), or simply replant one or more potatoes when you harvest the first batch. You cannot replant potatoes in open soil because of the risk of spreading disease, but in a container it matters less, as you will be replacing the soil with fresh potting compost the following season. You can use the spent compost in the garden, but not directly where you will be planting potatoes or tomatoes.

Harvesting from containers

Earlies take about thirteen weeks to grow, maincrops about 20 weeks. Very fast-growing earlies, such as Swift, may be ready in eleven weeks. If you are using a purpose-built potato barrel, you can slide open the panel to check the size of the potatoes. If you are growing them in a plastic bag, you should be able to check their size by feeling through the plastic. Otherwise, push your fingers gently into the compost and feel around. As a rough guide, the potatoes will be ready when the flowers start to fade or the stems begin to fall. For maincrops, cut the haulm and harvest the potatoes ten days later. Yields in containers can be very good – often better than from plants grown in open soil.

Companion planting

Companion planting is a planting scheme whereby you plant certain species together to enhance growth or ward off pests. Opinion is divided as to how much good it does, but one thing is certain: it does no harm. Above all, don't plant potatoes and tomatoes near each other: both are prone to blight. Other plants will help the potatoes by repelling pests. Flowers such as nasturtiums and marigolds will look pretty in between the rows, while also being useful. Horseradish will help in the fight against disease and also deters eelworms (but beware – the plants can get huge and are best planted at the edge of the potato patch). Nettles will also help, but you probably don't want to encourage them in your vegetable garden.

The potato guest list

Good companions	Bad companions
Aubergines	Cucumber
Celery	Jerusalem artichokes
Cabbage	Raspberries
Horseradish	Tomatoes
Peas and beans	Rosemary
Sweetcorn	Sunflowers
Alliums	Orache
Deadnettle	Many fruit trees, especially
Flax	apples and cherries
Foxgloves	
Marigolds	
Nasturtiums	

Problems

The best way to avoid problems is to make sure your plants are strong and happy. Practise crop rotation, put the plants far enough apart for the air to circulate easily, and provide adequate water throughout the growing season. Good, rich soil will ensure that potatoes are better able to fight off pests and diseases. Remember: prevention is always better than cure.

Blight

Maincrops are the most at risk from blight as the damp, humid conditions common in late summer are perfect for the fungal spores that cause it. The spores are carried by the wind, but rain can wash them down the plant and into the soil, where they will infect the tubers and cause them to rot.

   The first signs are patches that appear on the leaves: these are usually brown with paler edges. There will also be white fungal rings on the underside of the leaves. As soon as these signs appear, remove and destroy all the foliage. This may prevent the spores reaching the tubers. In theory, you can compost the foliage as long as the compost heap gets sufficiently hot (50°C/ 122°F); however, I don't like taking the risk of leaving any blight spores in the garden, so

I don't do it. If you have access to a flamethrower, it is a good way of destroying the tops of the plants, as it will kill any remaining spores.

Once you have cut off the haulm, the tubers will stop growing, but leave them in the ground for a couple of weeks to reduce the risk of the tubers being infected when you lift them. During this time, you will simply have to be patient and hope for the best.

Hideous as blight is, there are preventive measures you can take. Avoid overhead watering, and instead apply water at the base of the plant or on the surrounding soil. Earthing up will provide some protection. You can also spray with copper fungicide at two-weekly intervals from midsummer onwards. Bordeaux mixture, in small quantities, is approved as an organic method, but the copper it contains is toxic and any build-up is harmful to earthworms.

Scab

Scab also only tends to affect maincrop potatoes. This bacterial disease produces raised scabs on the tubers, which are unsightly and give the skin an unpleasant taste, but they can usually be removed by peeling. Scab is common in hot, dry summers and tends to be worst on free-draining, alkaline soil.

The best plan is prevention. Dig in plenty of organic matter the previous autumn, to help the soil retain water. Avoid mushroom compost, or any mixtures containing lime. Put grass cuttings or comfrey leaves in the planting trench to help keep the soil moist, and ensure that the soil is kept damp.

Blackleg

The telltale signs of blackleg are that the upper leaves roll and wilt, and the stems turn black and rot at the base. The tubers may also rot. Remove the affected plants immediately and do not store the tubers, even if they look all right. Blackleg is worst in wet summers, when the soil becomes waterlogged. It is most common in earlies that have been stressed by conditions that are too cold and wet. Dig in plenty of organic matter and, if necessary, add grit to ensure that the soil drains properly.

Viruses

There are a multitude of viruses that can affect potatoes and if they were all listed here, you would never grow another potato again. In most cases, the leaves roll inwards or develop mosaic patterns and the yields are poor. Good garden practices will reduce the plants' susceptibility and, increasingly, virus-resistant varieties are becoming available.

Slugs

The slugs that attack potatoes are keeled slugs, which live below the surface of the ground. Nematodes are very effective, although they can work out expensive over large areas. Follow the instructions and don't spread them too thinly. Slugs tend to be worst in heavy soil, especially towards the end of summer. Digging in plenty of well-rotted manure the previous autumn will discourage them. Surface slugs can be deterred by fine grit or coffee grounds spread in a ring around the stems.

Potato cyst eelworm

Potato cyst eelworms live in the soil. They lay eggs that can remain dormant for up to ten years, and the young eelworms eat the roots of the plants. The plants become weak, the leaves wilt and the tubers remain tiny. There is no cure and once a plant is infected, all you can do is pull it up and destroy it. Crop rotation is the best defence against eelworms. You cannot plant potatoes where there has been a serious infestation, but planting a crop of *Sinapis alba*, a mustard green manure, will help to clear them. Horseradish will also get rid of them.

Wireworms

Wireworms are usually only a problem on freshly cultivated land and are soon eliminated with continuous cultivation. Once the soil has been turned, the worms are exposed and birds will quickly eat them. The 2.5cm (1in) brown worms tunnel into the tubers and riddle them with holes. The best defence is to dig the soil well the autumn before planting potatoes for the first time.

Colorado beetle

The Colarado beetle originated in North America and has now spread to all parts of Europe except Britain and Ireland. The very distinctive yellow-and-black-striped beetles eat the foliage of potato plants. If you should see any, destroy the plants immediately and inform the authorities (see the DEFRA website at www.defra.gov.uk for more details).

Harvesting

As a general rule, you can harvest first earlies in early summer to midsummer, second earlies in late summer to early autumn, and maincrops in early to mid-autumn. You need to have finished the harvest by the time of the first frost, and the golden rule – for all potatoes – is to collect them all. Any that you leave in the ground may grow and possibly infect future years' harvests. You should also discard any green ones, as they are potentially harmful. Dig gently, using a flat-tined fork (properly known as a spud), as this is less likely to damage the tubers.

Earlies

With earlies, when a plant flowers, it is a good indication that the potatoes beneath are ready to harvest. Most will be ready when the flowers are fully open or the buds are beginning to drop, but some may be earlier, so it is worth feeling gently in the ground with your fingers. If you are growing the plants in open soil, push in a fork about 30cm (12in) away and gently dig up the whole plant. If you are growing the potatoes under plastic, simply remove the covering and you will find the potatoes lying on the surface of the ground. Potatoes growing in containers can be tipped out or dug up.

Most first earlies are best eaten straight away, so harvest them as and when you want to eat them. Within an hour of being dug up, the starch in the potatoes begins to turn to sugar, which can spoil the taste, so it is best to take them straight from the ground to the table.

Maincrops

Maincrop potatoes benefit from being left in the ground as long as possible, but you need to balance that against the risk of an early frost or a wet autumn and slug damage. As autumn progresses, the foliage will start to die down. You can either leave it as it is, or cut the haulm back to about 5cm (2in). Leave the tubers in the ground for another 10–14 days to allow their skins to harden, so they will keep better.

Choose a dry, sunny day and dig up the potatoes as you would earlies, bearing in mind that the tubers may have spread over a wider area. Lay the potatoes on the surface of the ground and leave them to dry for a couple of hours, turning them over so all the sides dry. Gently remove any large lumps of earth, but don't clean the potatoes; they actually store better with a bit of mud around them. If you have to harvest the potatoes on a wet day, spread them out indoors and do not store them until they are properly dry.

Storage

The best potatoes for storing are floury maincrops and, if you grow enough, these will get you right through the winter to the arrival of new potatoes the following year. Some maincrops, such as Golden Wonder, actually taste better after a period of storage. Most early potatoes do not store well and are best eaten as soon as possible after you dig them up. If it is necessary to keep them for a longer period, put them in a paper bag in the larder or the salad drawer of the fridge, where they will be fine for a week or two.

Having said that, it is possible to store new potatoes for Christmas Day if you can't grow a late crop. Simply put the potatoes in a biscuit tin, packed round with damp sand. Bury the tin in the ground and leave undisturbed until you want them. The combination of dark and damp will keep the potatoes fresh and stop them sprouting.

Maincrops should be stored in paper or hessian sacks or in wooden boxes or on trays. These need to be kept in a cool, dark, frost-free place. The potatoes must be absolutely dry and not rotten or green. Some earth doesn't matter; if anything it will help preserve the flavour. Allow air to circulate and check the potatoes once a week to prevent any rot spreading. Store away from strong smells such as chemicals, petrol or onions (although potatoes and onions should not be stored together anyway, because onions need light and potatoes need dark).

If you have space outside, a potato (or root) clamp is an old but efficient way of storing potatoes. The best place to make one is usually on top of the area where the potatoes have been growing, as you won't need to plant the next crop in the rotation until spring. Choose a dry period and flatten the ground. Spread a thick layer of straw or shredded newspaper, to act as insulation, and pile up the potatoes in a flattish mound. The straw and potatoes must be absolutely dry. Cover the potato mound with more straw and then dig the surrounding soil and pack that on top of the straw to a depth of about 10–15cm (4–6in). This will insulate the

clamp and raise it above the surrounding ground. Leave the top open for a few days to release any moisture. Cover the top with a layer of straw, like a thatched roof, and add a final layer of earth. The potatoes will be safe from rain and frost, but a clamp is not rat-proof. If you want to separate different varieties, make a long clamp and mark it into divisions. As and when you want some potatoes, simply remove the soil and straw, take out what you want and replace the protective layers. When all the potatoes have been used, you can simply dig the straw into the earth.

Varieties

There are hundreds of varieties of potato to choose from in Britain. Some are common and easy to find, while others are rare and only available from specialist sources. There are heritage varieties and new breeds, each with their own characteristics. Strictly speaking, the different potatoes are cultivars, rather than varieties, but they are generally referred to as varieties by gardeners and in catalogues. Potatoes are usually referred to by their cultivar name rather than the Latin, eg Anya, King Edward. Botanically these should be written within single inverted commas, but these are frequently omitted for ease of reading, as we have done in this book.

What do you want to eat? Waxy and floury potatoes perform very differently in the kitchen and it is important to grow what you will find useful. Taste is obviously crucial, but large-scale tests show that this is

highly subjective; if you look at four different references, you are quite likely to find four completely different recommendations. For this reason, the descriptions below do not include remarks on flavour: my preferences may not be yours. Potato Days (see page 94) are often a good place to test varieties and see which you like. Texture, skin colour, flesh colour and shape may also be a consideration. If you want the plants to look pretty, you will also need to find out what the flowers are like.

Coloured potatoes

Coloured potatoes are fun, but the flesh of some types turns an unattractive grey when cooked and there are only so many blue chips you can serve. Many early breeders concentrated on red or white potatoes, as they felt that these would be more acceptable to an already unenthusiastic market.

Good coloured varieties are becoming increasingly available from specialist breeders: Collessie (purple), Highland Burgundy Red (red), Salad Blue (blue) and Vitelotte (purple) all retain their extraordinary colours if steamed in their skins. Others have wonderful names such as Purple Congo, Cardinal, Urenika, Port Wine Kidney, Maori Chief, Egyptian Red, Canada Black, Moe Moe and Peru Peru, and are worth growing in small quantities if you can find supplies.

Heritage and modern potatoes

Finally, do you want to grow heritage varieties or modern ones? Until fairly recently, everyone trusted science and new varieties were eagerly awaited. Now, with some justification, we are more sceptical, and heritage varieties are becoming more popular. These pre-1950 varieties have been tried and tested for generations. Many are easy to grow, robust and delicious. Old varieties may have historical charm, but not all modern ones are boring and characterless. Many new varieties have disease resistance bred in, which makes it easier for the gardener to avoid pesticides (which were often used with gay abandon on potatoes in the past). Many old varieties died out because a better alternative came along. Others have stood the test of time. Consider everything. If you have the space, grow the varieties that you know you like, but set aside a small area each year to try something new.

All varieties have good and bad points. The common varieties, such as Charlotte and Picasso, may be everywhere but they have earned their popularity by being easy to grow, tasty (in most people's opinion!) and reliable. Heritage varieties may be vulnerable to disease but can taste fantastic, and you have the added bonus of growing a truly historical vegetable. Modern varieties, such as the unromantically named BF15, may seem anonymous but will probably have better pest and disease resistance and often taste delicious. The RHS carries out regular trials at their gardens around the country, and the RHS Award of Garden Merit (indicated by 'AGM' or the symbol of a trophy cup on the label) is a good indicator of all-round quality.

The potatoes listed on pages 52–57 are just a few of the ones you will find. There is a mixture of old and modern, floury and waxy, earlies and maincrops. Remember that growing times vary according to local conditions, and second earlies may be variously described as first earlies or maincrops. Few varieties are impervious to pests and diseases, but many of them have good levels of resistance. Dates and place of origin are given, where known.

Potato varieties

Accent
First early. Origin: Netherlands, 1989. Waxy.
A very early variety, with high yields of yellow, medium-sized tubers. Good resistance to eelworms, slugs and scab.

Amandine
First early. Origin: France, 1994. Waxy.
Cross between Mariana and Charlotte. Gives high yields of pale yellow salad potatoes, which also bake well.

Annabelle
First early. Origin: UK, 2001. Waxy.
Cross between Nicola and Mona Lisa. Plants are compact and grow well in containers, giving high yields of potatoes with pale skins and yellow flesh.

Anya
First (or second) early. Origin: Scotland, 1995. Waxy.
Cross between Desirée and Pink Fir Apple, and combines the good points of each parent. Harvested earlier than Pink Fir Apple, so is less at risk from blight, and is less knobbly, so easier to peel. Reliable, prolific and good in containers, producing attractive tubers with pinky-brown skins.

Arran Pilot
First early. Origin: Scotland, 1930. Waxy.
Gives good yields, especially in light soils and sheltered spots. Good disease resistance. Potatoes vary in size, which may be a good or bad thing, depending on your point of view.

Arran Victory
Late maincrop. Origin: Scotland, 1918. Floury.
Grows into a bushy, tall plant and takes time to mature, but has some resistance to blight. Tubers have purply-blue skin and white flesh. Makes especially good mash.

Belle de Fontenay
Early maincrop. Origin: France, 1885. Waxy.
Old French variety that produces small, kidney-shaped tubers. At risk from slugs, but matures early so is less at risk from blight. A good salad potato and stores well.

BF15
Second early (early maincrop). Origin: France, 1947. Waxy.
Cross between Belle de Fontenay and Flava. Gives high yields of large, oval tubers with yellow flesh.

Blue Danube (Adam Blue)
Early maincrop. Origin: Uncertain. Floury.
Plant is tall with blue flowers; foliage only has partial blight resistance, but tubers are better. Potatoes have bright, bluey-purple skins and white flesh, and bake very well.

Dyslexic
Recipe
for fish.

WE CAN MAKE
TOGETHER THE DIFFERENCE
Road Safety

white fillets. + salt &
pepper.
Fry in hot oil for aprox
3 min skin side down.
Turn & fry for aprox 2 min

Melt 1oz butter in pan
& spoon over fish with
marinade
salt & pepper
1 bunch flat leaf parsley
12-15 fresh basil leaves
1 clove garlic chopped fine
1 lemon with zest & peel fine
+ juice & oil (olive) to mix

Cara

Late maincrop. Origin: Ireland, 1976. Firm to floury.

A tough plant. Late-maturing, but has some resistance to blight, good general disease resistance and partial resistance to eelworms. Gives high yields of potatoes that store well.

Charlotte

Second early. Origin: France, 1981. Waxy.

Does well in containers, with pinky-violet flowers. Gives high yields of yellow potatoes, which are equally good hot or cold.

Collessie

Maincrop. Origin: Created by Bill Rollo, an amateur grower in Scotland, by crossing Pink Fir Apple and Shetland Black, date unknown.

Potatoes have smooth, near-black skins and purple flesh, retain their colour well when steamed with the skin on, and make truly amazing bright purple mash.

Concorde

First early. Origin: Netherlands, 1998. Waxy.

Gives high yields of large, oval tubers with pale yellow flesh. Good resistance to frost and partial resistance to eelworms and slugs.

Desirée

Early maincrop. Origin: Netherlands, 1962. Floury but firm.

Best on medium to heavy soil, where it gives high yields of tubers with pink skin and pale yellow flesh. Plants are compact, with pink and white flowers, and do well in containers. Good resistance to slugs and drought, but at risk from scab. Potatoes are particularly good for chips and baking.

Duke of York

First early. Origin: Scotland, 1891. Waxy at first, becoming increasingly floury as the season progresses.

The tubers can either be harvested as new potatoes or left to mature. The plant has attractive blue foliage and large white flowers.

Edzell Blue

Second early. Origin: Scotland, late Victorian. Floury.

Attractive white flowers and does well in containers, but at risk from eelworms. Potatoes have bluey-purple skins and white flesh. They tend to fall apart when boiled, so steam and use for mash.

Epicure

First early. Origin: UK, 1897. Floury.

Frost-resistant but prone to blight. The plant grows well in containers, giving high yields of knobbly potatoes with deep eyes.

Estima

Second early. Origin: Netherlands, 1973. Firm, holding together when boiled.

Does well in containers, giving high yields of large tubers. Drought-tolerant and resistant to slugs and blight, but scab can be a problem.

Foremost

First early. Origin: UK, 1954. Slightly waxy and firm.

Was originally called Sutton's Foremost. Resistant to slugs, gives good yields and has pretty white flowers. Holds together well when boiled and is good hot or cold.

Golden Wonder

Late maincrop. Origin: UK, 1906. Floury.

Originally used for Golden Wonder crisps. Matures very late; resistant to scab but at risk from slugs and drought. Plants are tall, with blue-violet flowers. Tubers can be small and yields low, but they store well. Can disintegrate when boiled, but make brilliant mash and chips.

Highland Burgundy Red

Early maincrop. Origin: Scotland, possibly 1930s. Floury.

The name may come from the fact that it was reputed to have been used for a dinner for the Duke of Burgundy at the Savoy Hotel in 1936. According to Alan Romans, this variety may be the same as Red Salad, Beetroot Tattie and Egyptian Red ('Egyptian' here meaning Romany gypsy, and exotic and colourful). The skin can be bright red when dug, but becomes a deeper burgundy as the potato ages. Flesh is a rich red, which can be preserved if the potatoes are steamed in their skins. Makes extraordinarily beautiful mash.

International Kidney (Jersey Royal)

Early maincrop. Origin: England, 1879. Waxy, becoming floury later.

Called the Jersey Royal when grown in Jersey and harvested as a new potato (do not confuse with the Jersey White, which is a Jersey-grown Maris Piper). Can be harvested before maturing as a second early, for a waxy salad potato; alternatively, can be left to mature into a larger floury maincrop. Plant does not like late frosts or wet summers.

Kerr's Pink

Late maincrop. Origin: Scotland, 1917. Floury.

A tall plant that does well on heavy, wet soil. Potatoes have attractive pink skins.

Kestrel

Second early. Origin: Scotland, 1992. Floury.

Good resistance to disease, eelworms and slugs. Tubers are large, with white skins and purple eyes.

King Edward

Early maincrop. Origin: England, 1902. Floury.

Originally called Fellside Hero,

but a clever merchant renamed it to capitalise on the publicity for the coronation of King Edward VII. Does well in containers, giving moderate yields, but susceptible to blight and drought. Potatoes have a cream skin with red patches and store well. They tend to fall apart when boiled, but are excellent for mash, roasting and chips.

Lady Christl
First early. Origin: Netherlands, 1996. Waxy.
Very early and gives good yields. Resistant to scab and eelworms, but likes a sheltered site and fertile soil.

Linzer Delikatess
Second early. Origin: Austria, 1976. Waxy.
Gives high yields of kidney-shaped potatoes that look like Jersey Royals but are not as special.

Maris Bard
First early. Origin: England, 1972. Waxy.
Very early, coming just after Rocket and Swift. Does well under cover, gives high yields, is drought-tolerant and has good disease resistance. Flowers are reddish-purple.

Maris Peer
Second early. Origin: England, 1962. Floury, but holds together well if harvested early in the season.
Grow the plants fairly close together, keep them well earthed up and you will get large numbers of small potatoes. Resistant to scab and blight, but susceptible to drought. Foliage is neatly rounded, with pretty purple flowers.

Maris Piper
Early maincrop. Origin: England, 1964. Firm to floury.
Gives high yields and has partial resistance to eelworms, but resistance to scab, slugs and drought is low, making it a poor choice for most gardeners. The potatoes are commercial favourites, especially in fish and chip shops.

Mimi
First early. Origin: Scotland, 2002. Waxy.
A very early, very compact plant, giving high yields of small potatoes. Will grow in a 20cm (8in) container. Potatoes have red skins and pink, marbled flesh, and look interesting when boiled whole.

Nadine
Second early. Origin: Scotland, 1987. Waxy.
Gives reliable yields, has resistance to eelworms and slugs, grows well in containers and has pinky-violet flowers.

Nicola
Early maincrop. Origin: Germany, 1973. Waxy.
Gives high yields, has eelworm resistance and some resistance to blight. Potatoes store well.

Pentland Dell
Early maincrop. Origin:
Scotland, 1961. Floury.
Gives high yields, but has scruffy-looking foliage. Bred as resistant to blight, but the disease has evolved, leaving it less so; however, it is resistant to slugs and drought. Potatoes tend to disintegrate when boiled, but are good for chips, roasting and baking.

Pentland Javelin
First early. Origin: Scotland,
1968. Waxy.
Takes time to mature and is one of the last first earlies. Gives high yields and is resistant to scab and golden eelworm.

Picasso
Second early (early maincrop).
Origin: Netherlands, 1992. Firm
and creamy.
Has resistance to scab, eelworms, blight and drought, and gives high yields. Potatoes have cream skins, with brilliant red eyes, and store well.

Pink Fir Apple
Late maincrop. Origin: France
or Germany, c.1850; grown in
England from the late nineteenth
century. Waxy.
Harvested late, so is prone to blight. Tubers spread, so leave plenty of space between plants and earth up gently. The long, knobbly tubers are pink with a white flesh, and have the true flavour of a new potato. Should be cooked in their skins (they are almost impossible to peel) and

are delicious in a salad or cooked whole as chips.

Ratte
Early maincrop. Origin: France,
1872 (although it may be the
same as the Danish variety,
Asparges). Waxy.
Does not give very high yields, but the long tubers are good in salads and store well. Plant is compact, with pretty purple flowers with bright yellow centres.

Red Duke of York
First early. Origin: Netherlands,
1942. Floury.
Generally healthy with low, bluish foliage and white flowers. Potatoes have bright red skins and pale yellow flesh, but skin fades when cooked.

Rocket
First early. Origin: England,
1987. Waxy.
Very early, and does well under cover or in containers. Fairly compact and the flowers are purple and bright yellow. Reasonable disease resistance but can be at risk from blight, so best harvested early.

Romano
Early maincrop. Origin:
Netherlands, 1978. Creamy;
similar to Desirée.
Resistant to scab and partially resistant to blight and eelworms, but drought-intolerant. Potatoes are red-skinned with white flesh and store well. Traditionally, Romano potatoes were used for gnocchi in Italy.

Roseval
Early maincrop. Origin: France, 1950. Waxy.
Very tall plant with attractive foliage, rich red stems and reddish-purple flowers. Potatoes have attractive pinky-red skin and yellow flesh.

Salad Blue
Early maincrop. Origin: uncertain. Firm and dense; floury.
Flowers are white and violet-blue with yellow anthers and the pollen is almost black. The blue skin and flesh of the potatoes is retained if they are steamed. They look odd but interesting in salad and as chips or mash. Salad Red is similar, but pink.

Sante
Early maincrop. Origin: Netherlands, 1983. Firm and creamy.
Robust plant with good resistance to slugs, eelworms and blight.

Shetland Black
Second early. Origin: Shetland, pre-1923. Floury.
The Shetland Islanders claim that this variety was rescued from a sunken Armada ship in 1588. The potatoes have dark blue skins and pale flesh with a purple ring. They make interesting chips and sautéed potatoes, but tend to go an off-putting bluish-grey when mashed.

Swift
First early. Origin: Scotland, 1994. Waxy.
Very early, with high yields of fewer, larger tubers than Rocket. Good resistance to disease and eelworms. Foliage is compact and plants do well in containers.

Valor
Late maincrop. Origin: Scotland, 1993. Creamy.
Gives high yields, even on poor soil, resistant to slugs and eelworms and generally has good resistance to disease, including blight. Potatoes store well.

Vitelotte (also known as Negresse or Truffe de Chine)
Late maincrop. Origin: seems to have first appeared in France but may have been growing in Peru or Bolivia in the 1800s. Floury.
This variety (or possibly varieties, as they are often listed separately) produces potatoes with dark purple skins and flesh. The best way to retain the colour is to steam unpeeled; makes extraordinary-looking chips, baked potatoes and mash.

Wilja
Second early. Origin: Netherlands, 1967. Firm and dry.
Gives high yields and does well in containers. Some resistance to blight, scab, blackleg and slugs.

Yukon Gold
Second early. Origin: Canada, 1980. Floury.
Potatoes have attractive golden skins and a buttery flavour.

Potatoes in the kitchen

Choosing the right variety

You can cook potatoes in almost any way and match them with a huge variety of flavours. The only way you cannot eat them is raw. Potatoes may all look roughly similar, but in culinary terms they can differ very considerably and it is important that you use the right variety for a particular purpose, otherwise you will get a different result from the one you were expecting.

For example, waxy potatoes can be mashed, but produce a purée rather than a fluffy mash. Waxy potatoes have a low water content, which means that they remain firm when boiled, as their cells stay together. This group includes new potatoes, which are available in early summer, and salad potatoes, which are available from early summer until autumn. These are the potatoes for boiling, salads, and gratins in which you want distinct layers.

Floury potatoes have a higher water content and more starch, and tend to collapse at the edges when boiled. This makes them perfect for roasting, as the fluffy edges absorb the oil and become crispy. They are also the best choice for baking and mashing. To find out what sort of potatoes you have, make a solution of 1 part salt to 11 parts water. A waxy potato will float in it, whereas a floury one will sink. In between are a range of potatoes which are variously described as creamy, firm, or all-purpose. These usually hold together well and can be used for most recipes, but some fall into the category of being an uninspiring jack-of-all-trades – adequate for most things, but brilliant at nothing.

The potato year

Potato dishes mirror the seasons: enjoy new potatoes with mint and butter, or in salads, for summer; create satisfying meals with baked potatoes, mash, roast potatoes and chips for autumn and winter. Many herbs and spices complement potatoes, and can be used fresh when in season. Try herbs such as bay, basil, chervil, chives, coriander, mint, parsley, rosemary, sage, tarragon and thyme. Spices such as chilli, cumin, garam masala, ginger and turmeric also work well.

Buying and storing potatoes

Unless you have a very large garden, you will probably need to buy potatoes at some stage in the year. Ideally, buy loose, unwashed potatoes, as these have the best flavour. The skin of new potatoes should rub away; that of all others should be firm, with no sprouts or green patches. Irregular shapes don't matter at all – they simply mean that the potatoes grew crowded together, or in soil with an uneven texture.

If you buy potatoes in a plastic bag, take them out immediately. New potatoes can be kept for a few days in the bottom of the fridge, but all others should be kept somewhere cool, dark and dry.

New potatoes can be frozen, either with or without their skins. Cook until slightly undercooked, drain, toss in butter (and mint if you like) and freeze in a plastic bag. They will keep for up to three months. Alternatively, blanch for two minutes, rinse in cold water, dry and put in a plastic bag to freeze. They will keep for twelve months. It is best to cook frozen potatoes from frozen (unless large), in butter or water.

It is not really worth freezing other types of potato: frozen roast potatoes need to be deep-fried to taste any good, and frozen baked potatoes take 50 minutes in an oven, which seems pointless when it takes little over an hour to bake one fresh. Chips and potato croquettes can be frozen, but commercially produced ones are so good that it hardly seems worth the hassle.

A word on the recipes

Regard the recipes in this book as a starting point, altering them as you wish. Many of the quantities are deliberately vague so you can use the amount you like. Most are for four people, but some – for example the salad – suggest four to six people (this depends on what else you are serving and, of course, how greedy your diners are). I use large eggs, and ideally these should be free-range and organic. For dairy products, I use full-cream milk and unsalted butter. For parsley, I prefer the flat-leaved type.

In most cases you can use whatever fat you like for frying: different oils, butter and dripping all have their own supporters. Equally, the amount of fat you use is, within reason, up to you, and may depend on the type of pan. I have a very elderly frying pan that seems to soak up butter before I've even started cooking.

Always test oven-cooked dishes, as individual ovens can vary considerably.

Boiled potatoes

The basics

There are two questions here: whether or not you should peel potatoes, and whether it is better to steam or boil them. New potatoes should simply be gently scrubbed to remove the loose skin; small waxy potatoes are best left in their skins; for large floury potatoes, peeling is a matter of preference. Most of the flavour is not in the skin, but just beneath it, as are some vitamins. A good way to preserve both is to remove the skin after the potatoes have been cooked, because then only a very thin layer comes away. However, it's not easy to peel hot potatoes. A compromise is to serve the potatoes with their skins intact and let people peel their own if they wish.

There is an argument that steaming potatoes, rather than boiling them, keeps them firmer, preserves their vitamins and intensifies their flavour. This is all probably true, but as potatoes take longer to cook than most other vegetables, it usually makes sense to boil them in the bottom part of the steamer, and steam other vegetables above them.

Boiling maincrop potatoes

Cut the potatoes into chunks of a similar size. If you make them roughly the size of an egg, it ensures that the centre will get cooked through without the outer edges turning to mush. It is important that all the pieces are around the same size so that they will cook in the same amount of time. If you are preparing the potatoes ahead of time, put them into a pan of cold water to prevent them discolouring. Advance preparation will not spoil the flavour, but the longer the potatoes soak in water, the more vitamin content they will lose. Good varieties to use are firm maincrops such as Desirée, Estima, Maris Peer, Maris Piper and Romano.

Start the potatoes off in either cold or boiling water, which has been salted. Cold water allows the potatoes to absorb some of the water, which makes them juicer and less likely to break up. If you use boiling water, the potatoes will be cooking for a shorter time, which can preserve their flavour.

Cook until tender in water that is boiling, but not too furiously, as this will bash the potatoes about and cause them to break up. The cooking time depends on the size of the chunks – probably about 15–20 minutes. When they are done, the point of a sharp knife should slide in easily. Drain the potatoes, return them to the pan and put back on the hob briefly to steam off any remaining water. Add a knob of butter and stir gently so all the potatoes are coated. If you need to keep the potatoes warm, cover the pan with a clean cloth or newspaper rather than a lid. This will allow the steam to escape and stop the potatoes becoming soggy.

Bubble and squeak

Until the end of the nineteenth century, bubble and squeak was made of cold roast beef, onions and cabbage. After that time, potatoes gradually replaced the meat. Cabbage, kale or sprouts all work equally well in this recipe. The name comes from the noise the mixture makes in the pan while cooking.

SERVES 4

500G (1LB 2OZ) FLOURY POTATOES, COOKED
250G (9OZ) CABBAGE OR SPROUTS, COOKED AND FINELY CHOPPED
60G (2OZ) BUTTER OR BEEF DRIPPING
1 MEDIUM ONION, FINELY CHOPPED
SALT AND PEPPER

The potatoes need to be boiled until tender and then either roughly broken up or mashed – it depends on how smooth you want the bubble and squeak to be. If mashing, do not add too much milk or butter, as you need a firm consistency.

Mix the potatoes and greens and season with salt and pepper. Melt half the fat in a large frying pan and fry the onion until it is tender. Add the onion to the potato mixture and stir well.

Melt the remaining fat in the pan, tip in the potato mixture and flatten it (you can either flatten it across the pan, or split the

AU BON MARCHÉ – PARIS

CLASSE   BEN MON VIEUX , QUAND NOUS AURONS MANGÉ TOUT ÇA

mixture into individual patties. Small patties will hold together and
are easier to turn, whereas a single spread will break up and give a
more crumbly effect). Fry the mixture for a few minutes on each
side over a medium heat, until heated through and golden and
crispy on the outside.

65

Boiled new potatoes

New potatoes are very special. They can be used in the same way as any waxy or salad potato, but are instantly recognisable by their flaky skins. Jersey Royals are the ultimate new potato to buy: they are grown by a cooperative of growers in Jersey and the island climate and soil combine to produce a truly delicious potato. However, good as they may be, nothing will rival a new potato freshly dug from your garden. The first new potatoes are best served simply – with a little mint and a lot of butter.

SERVES 4
800G (1¾LB) NEW POTATOES
SPRIG OF MINT
BUTTER
SALT

Wash the potatoes and scrub to remove any loose skin. Bring a pan of water to the boil (to retain their flavour, new potatoes need to go into boiling water). Add the mint and a pinch of salt.

Put the potatoes in the pan, bring back to the boil, cover and boil until cooked (about 20 minutes). When they are done, the point of a sharp knife should slide in easily. Drain and return to the pan, holding it briefly over the heat to allow all the water to evaporate. Serve with a generous lump of butter.

Smashed new potatoes

*Smashed new potatoes retain their texture while being a perfect 'mop'
for any sauce (if simply mashed, they tend to become a slimy purée).*

SERVES 4

1KG (2¼LB) NEW OR WAXY POTATOES, SCRUBBED,
  AND PEELED IF YOU WISH
100G (3½OZ) BUTTER
1 TBSP CHOPPED ROSEMARY OR THYME
SALT AND PEPPER

Bring a saucepan of water to the boil, add the potatoes with a
pinch of salt, and cook for 15–20 minutes, until tender. Melt the
butter in a small saucepan and add the herbs.

Remove the potatoes from the heat, drain and cut up roughly,
using a knife. Be careful that the skins do not cluster together in
an unattractive lump. Add the potatoes to the butter and mix well.
Season with salt and pepper to taste.

Mashed potatoes

There are various implements for mashing potatoes: some people swear by a fork, many like a potato masher, while others use a potato ricer or electric mixer. Don't use a food processor, as this will turn the mash into a gluey wallpaper paste.

To make a good mash, use any floury potato. Cut the potatoes into smallish chunks, place in a saucepan of cold water with a pinch of salt and bring to the boil. Boil until cooked, probably about 20 minutes. Drain, return to the pan to allow all the steam to escape, then mash with a good knob of butter, warm mik and seasoning.

Variations
Freshly grated nutmeg: Add at the end instead of pepper.
Cheese: Add grated cheese at the end and beat well. Cheddar will give you a very smooth, cheesy mash; Parmesan will add a cheese flavour but alter the texture less.
Coarse-grained mustard: Mustard mash makes a perfect accompaniment to sausages. Add the mustard, a teaspoonful at a time, towards the end and beat in well. Be careful not to overpower the flavour of the potatoes.
Fried onion: Slice an onion thinly and fry until transparent. Mix into the potatoes at the end.
Spring onions: Chop finely and mix in towards the end.
Rocket, parsley or chives: Chop finely and beat in towards the end.
Garlic: A few cloves in the milk, while it warms, will give a mild, garlicky flavour to the mash.

Champ or chappit tatties

*In Ireland, champ was traditionally made at Hallowe'en or on All Souls'
Day, and offered to the fairies to ensure their goodwill. Bowls were left on
field posts or in the hedgerows under hawthorn or whitethorn bushes.*

SERVES 4

1KG (2¼ LB) FLOURY POTATOES, UNPEELED, CUT INTO CHUNKS
150G (5OZ) BUTTER
150ML (5FL OZ) MILK OR CREAM
6–8 SPRING ONIONS, FINELY CHOPPED
HANDFUL OF CHIVES, SNIPPED
SALT AND PEPPER

Put the potatoes in a saucepan of cold water, with a pinch of salt,
and bring to the boil. Boil until cooked (about 20 minutes). Drain,
return to the pan and hold briefly over the heat to allow all the
moisture to evaporate. Meanwhile, heat the milk, but do not allow
it to boil. Put the spring onions in the hot milk and leave to infuse
for 10 minutes or so.

Remove the skin. If the potatoes are too hot to handle (which
they will be unless you wear rubber gloves) hold the potato in
place with a fork and remove the skin with the point of a sharp
knife. Mash with the butter. The amount of butter and milk you
add will determine the consistency of the mash. If in doubt, add a
little at a time.

Pour the milk over the potatoes and beat with a wooden
spoon. Add the chives, and salt and pepper to taste.

Potato cakes

Potato cakes are very versatile and will go with many more things than the variations listed below. Just remember not to overpower the potato flavour with too many additions: this is not an excuse to empty the contents of your fridge into a bowl of mash and fry it. Use any floury potatoes for the mash. It should be fairly firm, so just make it with butter, rather than adding milk or cream.

SERVES 4

500G (1LB 2OZ) STIFF MASHED
  POTATO, COOLED (600G/1LB 5OZ
  POTATOES MAKES ROUGHLY THIS
  QUANTITY OF MASH) (SEE PAGE 68)

50G (1¾OZ) PLAIN FLOUR

25G (1OZ) MELTED BUTTER, PLUS
BUTTER FOR FRYING

1 EGG, BEATEN (OPTIONAL)

SALT AND PEPPER

Gradually mix the flour into the
mashed potato and season with salt and pepper. Stir in the melted butter. The dough should hold together without being too sticky. Add the egg to bind the mixture together if necessary.

    Put the mixture on a floured worktop and flatten into rounds with your hands. The size you make them is up to you, but anything bigger than a saucer tends to be a bit unwieldy. Make the potato cakes as level as possible, so the edges will crisp up when you cook them.

Melt a little butter in a heavy-bottomed frying pan or griddle and cook over a medium heat, turning once, so both sides are golden brown. Don't be tempted to fiddle with the potato cakes, otherwise the mixture will fall apart.

Variations

Herbs: To impart a delicate herby flavour, add thyme, rosemary, tarragon, sage or marjoram to the mixture.

Goat's cheese (hard): Crumble into the mixture, or cut into small chunks and add. It will melt inside the potato cake and give it a sharpness to contrast with the gentle flavour of the potato. Rosemary goes well with this.

Chives: A handful of snipped chives will sharpen the flavour of the potato cake without altering its texture.

Blue cheese: Crumble Stilton or any fairly hard blue cheese into the mash. I find soft cheeses alter the texture of the potato cake too much.

Leeks or onion: Chop finely, fry and add to the mixture.

Bacon: Grill or fry, chop and then mix with the potatoes as you mash them. You may find that you now need less melted butter. Thyme goes well with this combination.

Apple farls: Thinly roll out two potato cakes on a well-floured surface and cover one with thinly cut slices of peeled apple. Put the other cake on top and push down so they stick together. Fry on a griddle, turning once, so both sides are golden. Serve with melted butter and sugar.

Fishcakes

You can use almost any fish for these fishcakes: haddock (smoked or unsmoked), cod, salmon, or a mixture. Small prawns also work well.

SERVES 4
500G (1LB 2OZ) FISH
250ML (9FL OZ) MILK, SUFFICIENT TO COVER THE FISH IN THE PAN
BAY LEAF
500G (1LB 2OZ) STIFF MASHED POTATO (SEE PAGE 68)
HANDFUL OF HERBS (TRY PARSLEY, DILL OR CHERVIL), CHOPPED
1 EGG, BEATEN
FLOUR OR BREADCRUMBS SUFFICIENT TO COAT THE FISHCAKES
OIL OR BUTTER, FOR FRYING
SALT AND PEPPER
1 LEMON, CUT INTO WEDGES, TO SERVE

Put the fish in a shallow pan with the milk and bay leaf, so the milk just covers the fish. Boil until the fish turns opaque (this will take 5–10 minutes, depending on the fish). Remove from the pan and break into flakes, discarding any skin and bones.

Add the fish to the potato and mix well. Toss the herbs into the mixture and season to taste. Form into eight fishcakes. Dip each fishcake into the beaten egg and then roll it gently in the flour or breadcrumbs until all the sides are covered.

Heat a little oil or butter in a heavy-bottomed frying pan and cook over a medium heat, turning once, so both sides are golden. As with other potato cakes, don't be tempted to fiddle with them, or the mixture will fall apart. Serve with the lemon wedges.

Rösti

*These Swiss potato cakes should be light, crispy, soft and rich. They
make great accompaniments to any meal or can be eaten as a snack.
Many recipes recommend that you parboil the potatoes first, but if you
make the patties reasonably thin, it isn't necessary and this way you
preserve the grated texture of the potato (if you prefer to parboil, cook
for 7 minutes and then allow to cool). Use firm maincrop potatoes.*

SERVES 4
3 OR 4 LARGE POTATOES, PEELED
4 RASHERS OF STREAKY BACON, CHOPPED AND FRIED UNTIL CRISPY
HANDFUL OF THYME, CHOPPED (OPTIONAL)
4 TBSP VEGETABLE OR OLIVE OIL
115G (4OZ) BUTTER
SALT AND PEPPER

Grate the raw potatoes with a coarse grater. Spread the grated
potato on a tea towel and wring out to remove as much moisture
as possible. Mix the potato with the bacon and thyme (if using),
and season with salt and pepper. Divide the mixture into four and
flatten into patties.

   Heat the oil and butter in a heavy-bottomed frying pan. Slide
each patty into the pan and flatten with a spatula. Leave for a few
minutes and when the base is brown, flip on to the other side. Do
not flip the rösti too soon, as the patties will simply fall apart.
Depending on the size of the frying pan, you may be able to cook
all four at once, but if not, transfer the cooked ones to a warm
serving dish while cooking the remainder. Serve immediately.

Baked potatoes

A baked potato is probably one of the easiest meals in the world. You simply put it in the oven (pierced so it doesn't explode), leave it, take it out a bit later, cut it open and serve with butter, salt and pepper. That is all there is to it. There is also a wealth of fillings to choose from.

ALLOW 1 LARGE UNPEELED POTATO PER PERSON

TO SERVE
BUTTER
SALT

Preheat the oven to 200°C/400°F/gas mark 6. (You can bake potatoes at anything from 180°C/350°F/gas mark 4 up to this temperature, depending on what else you are cooking. They will just take longer at a lower temperature.)

Wash the potatoes, dry them on a cloth and pierce three or four times with a fork to prevent them from exploding in the oven.

A skewer pushed right through the potato will speed up the cooking time a bit and, more importantly, ensure that the centre is cooked properly. Very large potatoes can be cut in half lengthways and brushed with oil: this halves the cooking time.

If you want the skin to be salty, rub a little sea salt on while it is still damp. If you like crispy skin, rub a little oil on it. For soft skin, wrap the potato in tinfoil.

Allow about an hour for a large potato to cook. Baked potatoes are very accommodating – you can leave them in the oven for much longer if necessary and no harm will come to your meal. As soon as you take the potato out of the oven, cut it open (either with a cross or in two halves) to allow the steam to escape.

Serve with a sprinkling of salt and a generous lump of butter, or add a filling.

Good fillings for baked potatoes

Cottage cheese or soured cream with chives • Sweetcorn and grilled bacon • Avocado and grilled bacon • Any type of cheese – such as garlic cream cheese, goat's cheese, blue cheese or Parmesan – with chutney • Hummus with finely chopped spring onions • Crème fraîche, Parmesan and sage • Onions, finely sliced and fried, with finely chopped grilled bacon • Salsa • Leftover curry • Prawns and mayonnaise

Crispy roast potatoes

Goose or duck fat is the ultimate fat to use for roast potatoes, because it gives a lovely flavour. However, if you parboil the potatoes and rough up their edges, you will get excellent results using lard, dripping or olive oil. Choose a floury variety such as Golden Wonder, Maris Piper or Pentland Dell; or a firm all-rounder such as Desirée, Estima or Romano. New potatoes don't roast well because they have a high water content.

SERVES 4, GENEROUSLY
1KG (2¼ LB) POTATOES, PEELED
FAT, TO FORM A THIN LAYER
HANDFUL OF HERBS SUCH AS
    ROSEMARY, SAGE OR THYME
    (OPTIONAL)
SALT

Preheat the oven to 200°C/400°F/gas mark 6. Put the fat in the roasting tray and place it in the oven to heat.

Cut the potatoes into smallish chunks. Put them in a saucepan of salted boiling water and parboil for 4–5 minutes. Drain the potatoes and return to the saucepan, holding it briefly over the heat. Give the pan a good shake so the edges are roughened.

Remove the roasting tray from the oven and put the potatoes in it, with the herbs, if using. Be careful as the fat will be hot and may spit. Ensure that everything is well coated with fat. Return to the top shelf of the oven and cook for 40–50 minutes until golden brown and crispy. Turn the potatoes halfway through the cooking time to ensure that all sides brown.

Hedgehog potatoes

*These are probably better known as hasselback potatoes, but due to
a misunderstanding by the child of one of my recipe testers, they have
become Hedgehog Potatoes. They originate in Sweden and fan out
prettily when cooked. Any variety of potato will do: small waxy ones
are a bit fiddly to cut and very large maincrops don't work well as you
don't want to have to cut the potato into chunks before slicing it, but
anything the size of a tablespoon is fine.*

SERVES 4

1KG (2¼ LB) POTATOES, PEELED OR UNPEELED
60G (2OZ) BUTTER, MELTED, OR 50ML (2 FL OZ) OLIVE OIL
SPRIGS OF ROSEMARY
SALT AND PEPPER

Preheat the oven to 200°C/400°F/gas mark 6. Cut slices across
each potato every 5mm (¼ in), making sure that you do not cut
right through the potato. This will give you crispy slices; for slices
with soft centres, make them 1 cm (½ in) wide.

Put the potatoes in a greased roasting tin and brush each one
with melted butter or oil, making sure that it goes right down into
the cuts. Push sprigs of rosemary into the cuts and season with
salt and pepper.

Place in the oven: the cooking time will depend on the size of
the potatoes, but allow about 45–55 minutes. As the potatoes
cook, they will fan open. Check halfway through that all the cuts
are well oiled.

Chips

In nineteenth-century France, chipped and fried potatoes were called pommes Pont-Neuf and sold by street vendors. They arrived in Britain in the 1870s, and today we know them as chips or french fries. To make great chips, you need to cook them twice. Use any floury or firm potato, or try Pink Fir Apple (fried whole) and Salad Blue for blue chips. Groundnut oil is best for frying, but you could also use sunflower or vegetable oil.

SERVES 4

4–5 LARGE POTATOES, PEELED
2 LITRES GROUNDNUT OIL

Cut the potatoes into chips and put them into a bowl of cold water. This will wash away some of the starch, and you can leave the potatoes soaking overnight, if you want. Drain the chips and pat dry.

Pour the oil into a large, deep pan and heat to 150°C (302°F). You can check the temperature by putting a chip in the oil: if it floats, surrounded by bubbles, the oil is ready. Put the chips in a basket and lower it into the fat, which will bubble furiously. Cook for 6–7 minutes until soft. Lift the chips out of the fat and allow to cool briefly (if you want, the chips can be cooled fully and kept in the fridge for up to three days at this stage).

Heat the oil to 180°C (356°F). Return the chips to the oil and fry for about another 5 minutes, until golden. Drain on paper and eat immediately.

Sautéed potatoes

This is a very good way of using up leftover boiled potatoes. The best fat is a mixture of butter and oil.

SERVES 4
700G (1½LB) POTATOES, PEELED OR UNPEELED
BUTTER AND OIL FOR FRYING

Put the potatoes in a pan of boiling water and cook for about 10–15 minutes. Allow to cool a little and then cut into discs.

Heat the butter and oil in a frying pan: the fat should just cover the base of the pan when melted. When the fat is bubbling, tip in the potatoes so they form a single layer. Reduce the heat slightly and cook until the undersides are golden, then turn. The potatoes will probably take about 10–15 minutes. Serve immediately.

Crisps

Crisps, known in America as chips, were invented in 1853 by George Crum, an American chef. He chopped the potatoes into wafer-thin slices, fried them, added salt and they were an immediate hit.

It is possible to make crisps at home, but you have to have the oil at exactly the correct temperature and cook the potatoes for exactly the right amount of time, otherwise you end up with burnt-tasting crisps or potato 'flappies', neither of which is good.

Hot lightning

This Dutch dish has many variations, and this recipe is based on one from the delightfully named book Roast Figs and Sugar Snow *by Diana Henry. It makes an excellent winter accompaniment to sausages or any pork cuts, especially roast joints. You can leave the skin on the potatoes, apples and pears: it gives an appetizing, rustic look.*

SERVES 6, GENEROUSLY

1KG (2¼LB) SMALL WAXY POTATOES, UNPEELED

250G (9OZ) SHARP EATING APPLES, UNPEELED

250G (9OZ) PEARS, UNPEELED

60G (2OZ) BUTTER

HANDFUL OF FRESH THYME, CHOPPED

SOFT LIGHT BROWN SUGAR, TO TASTE

SALT AND PEPPER

Preheat the oven to 170°C/325°F/gas mark 3. Cut the potatoes in half, or into small chunks. Core the apples and pears and cut them into chunks the same size as the potatoes.

Melt the butter in a heavy-bottomed pan and sauté the potatoes until just crispy. Add the fruit and mix well so that it is all coated with the butter. Scatter in the thyme, season with salt and pepper, and add sugar to taste. Put into a lidded casserole and cook in the oven for about 45 minutes.

Stir a couple of times during cooking to stop it sticking, and if the potatoes are a little too firm, add 50ml (2fl oz) water to steam them.

HOLLAND'S

APRIL 1913

TEN CENTS A COPY
ONE DOLLAR A YEAR

C COLES PHILLIPS

Gratin dauphinoise

This is the ultimate luxurious potato gratin. Originating in the Alps of the Dauphiné, there are innumerable variations: you can add cooked smoked fish, celeriac or leeks, cheese, mushrooms, onions, ham or bacon. If you spread the potatoes in a large dish, with about four layers of potato, you will get lots of crispy topping; a smaller dish will give you more of the soft, creamy layers underneath. The recipe calls for double cream: don't use single cream, as it will separate.

SERVES 4, GENEROUSLY
BUTTER TO GREASE
700G (1½LB) POTATOES, PEELED AND THINLY SLICED
2 CLOVES OF GARLIC, FINELY SLICED
350ML (12FL OZ) DOUBLE CREAM
SALT AND PEPPER

Preheat the oven to 200°C/400°F/gas mark 6. Butter the dish and arrange the potatoes in layers with a layer of garlic in the centre. Season each layer as you go.

Pour the cream over the potatoes, making sure it gets in between all the layers. It should reach to just below the top layer of potatoes.

Cook in the oven for about 1 hour, until the lower layers are soft and the top is golden and crispy. If you are using a deep dish, it may take longer to cook: cover loosely with foil if the top is browning too much.

Jansson's temptation

This Scandinavian dish is one of the ultimate comfort foods for winter. There is some debate about who Jansson was: possibly Erik Jansson, a devoutly religious Swede, who sailed to America in the eighteenth century. He lived a strict life but this was, apparently, the one thing he could not resist. Use any firm variety of potato to make it.

Serves 4–6

12–15 ANCHOVY FILLETS
2 LARGE ONIONS, FINELY SLICED
BUTTER TO FRY AND TO GREASE
1KG (2¼ LB) POTATOES, PEELED AND CUT INTO FINE SLICES
250ML (8FL OZ) DOUBLE CREAM
SALT AND PEPPER

Preheat the oven to 200°C/400°F/gas mark 6. If the anchovies are very salty, soak them for about 30 minutes. Fry the onions in a little butter until soft.

Butter a gratin dish and layer the ingredients. Ideally, the layers should be potato, onion, potato, anchovy, potato, onion, potato. However, it doesn't matter too much as long as you end with a layer of potato. Season as you go, but take care not to add too much salt.

Pour the cream over the mixture, making sure it gets right through all the layers. It should reach to just below the top layer of potatoes (add a little milk if necessary). Cook in the oven for about an hour. Cover with foil if it is browning too much.

The endlessly variable potato soup

This is a soup that can be dressed up or down as much as you wish: serve it plain and simple, make it more indulgent by using cream instead of milk, or give it a sharp tang with some rocket. The variations are endless, and there are some ideas below. Use an all-rounder variety of potato, as these are nice and firm.

SERVES 4

50G (2OZ) BUTTER
450G (1LB) POTATOES, PEELED AND CUT INTO 1CM (½IN) CHUNKS
100G (3½OZ) ONION, FINELY CHOPPED
600ML (1PINT) VEGETABLE OR CHICKEN STOCK
100ML (3½FL OZ) MILK OR CREAM
SALT AND PEPPER

Melt the butter in a saucepan and add the potatoes and onion. Season with salt and pepper and stir well. Cover with a lid and sweat over a low heat for about 10 minutes, until the potatoes and onion are cooked.

Heat the stock and add it to the vegetables. Remove from the heat and blend to the desired consistency. Heat the soup again, if necessary, and add the milk or cream. You can mix in the milk or swirl the cream artistically over the top.

Variations

Leek: Chop three leeks and add them to the potato at the beginning of the recipe. Omit the onion.

Bacon: Fry or grill some bacon and cut it into chunks. Add before or after blending the soup, depending on whether you just want the flavour of bacon or the texture as well.

Herbs: Thyme, tarragon, parsley or chives all complement this soup. Add a handful before blending and then sprinkle a few more herbs on top to serve.

Watercress: Take a bunch of watercress and roughly separate the stems and leaves. Chop the stems and add to the potatoes and onions before you sweat them. Add the leaves at the same time as the stock, reserving a few for decoration before serving. Omit the pepper and add a pinch of grated nutmeg at the end. A spoonful of crème fraîche, added at the end, makes a good alternative to the milk or cream.

Peas: Add 100g (3½oz) fresh or frozen peas at the same time as the stock and simmer until cooked.

Rocket: Add a handful of chopped rocket at the end. Replace the milk or cream with a spoonful of crème fraîche if you wish.

Parsley: Use a good-sized bunch weighing about 115g (4oz). Cook the stalks in the stock with the potatoes and add the leaves, chopped, at the end.

Potato, leek and cheese tartlets

These tartlets are a variation on homity pie, an open vegetable pie that was especially popular during rationing in the Second World War. These tartlets are tasty and filling, and can be served hot or cold. Use six 10cm (4in) tartlet tins or a 22cm (9in) tart tin. Waxy potatoes are the best variety to use, as they retain their shape.

SERVES 4–6

FOR THE PASTRY
200G (7OZ) PLAIN FLOUR
75G (2¾OZ) BUTTER
25G (1OZ) PARMESAN OR STRONG
  CHEDDAR CHEESE, GRATED
PINCH OF SALT

FOR THE FILLING
30G (1OZ) BUTTER
2 LEEKS, ABOUT 225G (8OZ) IN TOTAL,
FINELY SLICED
1 SMALL ONION, FINELY CHOPPED
350G (12OZ) POTATOES, UNPEELED
2 EGGS, BEATEN
150ML (5FL OZ) DOUBLE CREAM
80G (3OZ) MATURE CHEDDAR CHEESE, GRATED
80G (3OZ) PARMESAN CHEESE, GRATED
1 TSP FINELY CHOPPED THYME
SALT AND PEPPER

Preheat the oven to 200°C/400°F/gas mark 6. Sift the flour and salt into a bowl, add the butter and rub it in with your fingertips until the mixture resembles fine breadcrumbs. Stir in the cheese.

Add sufficient cold water (about 3 tbsp) to bring the mixture into a firm dough. Be careful not to add too much as it will make the pastry shrink when you bake it. Wrap in clingfilm and chill for 30 minutes. Roll out the pastry thinly on a floured board. Line the greased tartlet tins with pastry, laying it right up the sides to accommodate the filling. Prick the base with a fork and line the pastry cases with baking paper and baking beans to bake them blind.

Bake in the oven for 10 minutes. Take the tarts out and reduce the oven temperature to 180°C/350°F/gas mark 4. Remove the paper and baking beans and return the tarts to the oven for about 5 minutes to dry out. Remove the tarts from the oven but leave it on.

Melt the butter in a frying pan and gently sauté the leeks and onion. Put the potatoes in a saucepan of boiling water and cook until tender (about 20 minutes). Drain the potatoes and, as soon as they are cool enough to handle, peel them and cut into small cubes about 1cm (½in) big.

Whisk together the eggs and cream, mix in the cheeses, add the thyme and season with salt and pepper. Stir in the leeks, onion and potatoes and pour the mixture into the pastry case. The eggs will hold the vegetables in place as they cook. Bake for 25–30 minutes, until the exposed potatoes and leeks on the top are just turning brown.

Bacon and spinach salad

This salad is a meal in itself. Use waxy potatoes.

SERVES 4–6

1KG (2¼ LB) JERSEY ROYAL POTATOES, SCRUBBED

16 RASHERS OF STREAKY BACON, FRIED OR GRILLED UNTIL CRISPY

200G (7OZ) BABY SPINACH LEAVES, WASHED AND DRAINED

FOR THE DRESSING

2 DESSERTSPOONS BALSAMIC VINEGAR

JUICE OF 2 LEMONS

2 TSP DIJON MUSTARD

2–3 TBSP MAYONNAISE

2–3 TBSP CRÈME FRAÎCHE

3–4 TBSP OLIVE OIL

200G (7OZ) PARMESAN CHEESE, COARSELY GRATED OR SHAVED

PEPPER

Cook the potatoes in salted boiling water for about 15–20 minutes. Cut the cooked bacon into small pieces.

Make the dressing: mix the vinegar, lemon juice and mustard together. Add the mayonnaise and crème fraîche and mix. Add the olive oil and Parmesan, reserving a handful of the cheese for a garnish. Season with pepper to taste.

Drain the potatoes and cut into thick slices while still hot. Put the spinach in a bowl, and add the potatoes and bacon. Pour the dressing over the salad and mix gently. Leave for 10 minutes for the flavours to mix. Garnish with the reserved Parmesan.

Potato bread

The potato gives this bread a lovely chewy quality.

MAKES 1 LOAF

200G (7OZ) COLD MASHED POTATO, MADE WITHOUT BUTTER OR
  MILK
400G (14OZ) STRONG WHITE FLOUR (POSSIBLY MORE)
1 TSP SALT
7G SACHET EASY-BLEND DRIED YEAST
HANDFUL HERBS SUCH AS SAGE, ROSEMARY OR THYME, CHOPPED
  (OPTIONAL)
300ML (½ PINT) TEPID WATER
BUTTER OR OIL TO GREASE

Mix the potato, flour, salt and yeast together. Add the herbs (if
using), reserving a few. Pour in the water bit by bit and mix into a
dough. Knead on a floured surface until smooth and not too sticky.

Shape the dough into a round and put it in a greased bowl,
turning it so it is well coated. Cover with a damp tea towel and
leave in a warm place for an hour or so until it has doubled in size.

Punch the dough down as hard as you like and knead for
another minute. Grease a large baking tray and then shape the
dough into a loaf on the tray. Push the remaining herbs into the
top. When it cooks, the loaf will spread to cover about double the
area. Cover with a tea towel and leave for 30 minutes to rise again.

Preheat the oven to 230°C/450°F/gas mark 8. Cook the loaf
for 10 minutes and then reduce the oven temperature to
200°C/400°F/gas mark 6. Cook for another 20 minutes, until risen
and golden. Remove from the oven and cool on a wire rack.

National Trust kitchen gardens

In their heyday, many country houses would have had extensive kitchen gardens. These were labour-intensive but, until the early twentieth century, labour was cheap. After this time labour costs spiralled, imported food became readily available and many of the gardens fell into disrepair. Increasingly, however, values are changing and many of the kitchen gardens have been restored to their former glory.

Not all the gardens listed below have extensive collections of potatoes, but all grow interesting and inspirational vegetables. Further information on the gardens and their opening times can be found at www.nationaltrust.org.uk.

Apprentice House Quarry Bank Mill, Styal, Cheshire. The Apprentice House housed 100 child labourers who worked in the adjoining mill, built in 1784. In humble plots, the children who lived there grew food for themselves and for sale. The vegetable varieties grown today are the same as those grown in the eighteenth century, and no chemicals are used.

Arlington Court Barnstaple, Devon. The restoration of the walled kitchen garden began in 1990, with work on the greenhouses and plantings of vegetables, flowers and fruit.

Barrington Court Near Ilminster, Somerset. Deep double borders lead to a large walled kitchen garden with flower borders down the centre.

Bateman's Burwash, Sussex. The attractive kitchen garden in the orchard is planted with vegetables and annuals for cut flowers, and supplies the tea-room. There are also vegetables in the borders of the mulberry garden, planted as they would have been when Rudyard Kipling lived here.

Beningbrough Hall Yorkshire. The walled kitchen garden supplies the restaurant with vegetables and fruit.

Calke Abbey Ticknall, Derbyshire. The walled kitchen garden has been restored, with rotating beds of old varieties. The larger upper kitchen garden is now mainly grazed by sheep.

Chartwell Westerham, Kent. Home of Winston Churchill. The Golden Rose Avenue runs down the centre of the kitchen garden, glowing with yellow and gold roses given to Sir Winston and Lady Churchill by their children to celebrate their golden wedding anniversary.

Clumber Park Worksop, Nottinghamshire. The huge walled kitchen garden is organically managed, although the house has long since been demolished.

The Courts Garden Holt, Wiltshire. The recently restored kitchen garden includes vegetables, herbs, a nuttery, an orchard and an apple arch. Seasonal fresh produce is sold.

Felbrigg Hall Norwich, Norfolk. The large walled kitchen garden is a fully working garden, with vegetables, fruit, flowers and greenhouse grapes.

Fenton House Hampstead, London. This charming town house has a country-style orchard and vegetable garden.

Hill Top Hawkshead, Cumbria. This small house belonged to Beatrix Potter, the author, and you can easily imagine Peter Rabbit scurrying about among the neat rows in the small vegetable garden.

Hinton Ampner Bramdean, near Alresford, Hampshire. The walled garden has been restored as a productive area and produce and plants can be bought.

Hughenden Manor High Wycombe, Buckinghamshire. Disraeli's walled kitchen garden has been restored and has vegetables in containers and raised beds.

Knightshayes Court Tiverton, Devon. The Victorian walled garden has been restored and is run on organic principles, supplying fruit and vegetables for the restaurant.

Lindisfarne Castle Holy Island, Northumberland. Gertrude Jekyll laid out the garden but only specified 'vegetables', not specific varieties. In 2004 it was restored, using heritage varieties that were also attractive.

Little Moreton Hall Congleton, Cheshire. A pair of vegetable beds by the moat contain herbs and heritage vegetables.

Llanerchaeron Aberaeron, Ceredigion. This house had been in the Lewis family for ten generations and was in poor condition when it came to the Trust in 1989. Although the garden is on heavy clay, it has been continuously cultivated for so many years that the soil is now rich and crumbly. Many of the plants are grown in raised beds to counter the problem of high rainfall in this area. The vegetables grown include modern varieties of the types that the original gardeners would have chosen.

Oxburgh Hall Oxborough, near King's Lynn, Norfolk. The large kitchen garden has been converted into an orchard, although the impressive castellated walls and turrets remain. One area is run as a productive plot, with vegetables and cut flowers.

Sissinghurst Biddenden Road, near Cranbrook, Kent. The vegetable garden has recently been made in an adjoining field and was first open to the public in 2009. It is large and practical, rather than ornamental, and supplies the restaurant and shop.

Tatton Park Knutsford, Cheshire. The walled kitchen garden covers over 0.8 hectares (2 acres) and is divided into a four-bed rotation scheme.

Tintinhull Garden Tintinhull, Yeovil, Somerset. There is an attractive kitchen garden.

Trengwainton Garden Madron, near Penzance, Cornwall. There are five walled gardens, each built to the dimensions of Noah's Ark. The beds slope to provide good drainage and face west to make the most of the sunshine. Old accounts refer to new potatoes on New Year's Day. There are plans to plant part of the garden with new varieties, in keeping with Trengwainton's experimental traditions.

Tyntesfield Wraxall, Bristol, Somerset. This Victorian mansion has a large walled garden with glasshouses, an orangery and a central dipping pool.

Upton House near Banbury, Warwickshire. There is a large kitchen garden, which has been continuously cultivated since 1695. Hidden from the garden by a ha-ha, the beds are angled to face south and all the vegetables are grown on a four-year rotation system.

The Vyne Sherbourne St John, Hampshire. The walled garden has been restored as a productive garden, with vegetable beds and glasshouses that supply the restaurant.

Wimpole Hall Royston, Cambridgeshire. There is a walled kitchen garden with vegetables, flowers and espaliered fruit next to the Home Farm.

Wordsworth House and Garden Cockermouth, Cumbria. The walled garden is planted with varieties of flowers, fruits, herbs and vegetables that were grown in the 1770s, when the poet William Wordsworth lived there.

Potato Days

Every year, Garden Organic holds Potato Days at its garden at
Ryton in Warwickshire. These days are the ideal way to learn
more about the different varieties of potato you can grow. Over
100 varieties are available, often as individual tubers, and there
is advice on growing, cookery demonstrations and potato-based
food. Garden Organic started the events in the 1990s (when it
was the Henry Doubleday Research Association), and the idea
has now been taken up by many allotment societies, nurseries
and organic gardening groups. Potato Days are usually held
between January and March to coincide with planting times.
Visit the website www.potatoday.org for information about
events around the country.

Picture credits

pages 1, 25, 28, 33, 35, 36, 45, 47, 62, 76, 85 © Becca Thorne

pages 5, 75 © PoodlesRock/Corbis

page 10 Page from a school textbook illustrating the Cultivation of the Potato, c.1910 (colour litho) by French School. Private Collection/Archives Charmet/The Bridgeman Art Library

pages 13, 49, 65 Beryl Peters Collection/Alamy

page 16 *Potato picking* by English School, (20th century). Private Collection/© Look and Learn/The Bridgeman Art Library

pages 18, 23 Mary Evans Picture Library

page 22 Emilio Ereza/Alamy

page 50 Meriel Thurstan

page 81 Image courtesy of The Advertising Archives

Index